WHITEWATER RAFTING

EXCITING AND SAFE OUTDOOR FUN

David and Patricia Armentrout

A Crabtree Seedlings Book

CRABTREE
Publishing Company
www.crabtreebooks.com

T0020736

TABLE OF CONTENTS

WHITEWATER RAFTING

Imagine rafting slowly down a calm river, enjoying the scenery. Suddenly, someone yells "Get ready!" The water begins to flow faster and rougher, splashing your face.

You smile, dig your paddle in, and help your team through the **rapids.** You're whitewater rafting!

Whitewater rafting is exciting, adventurous, and can be hard work! Often there is a mix of calm waters with stretches of fast-moving rapids.

Rapids can appear as white, turbulent water.

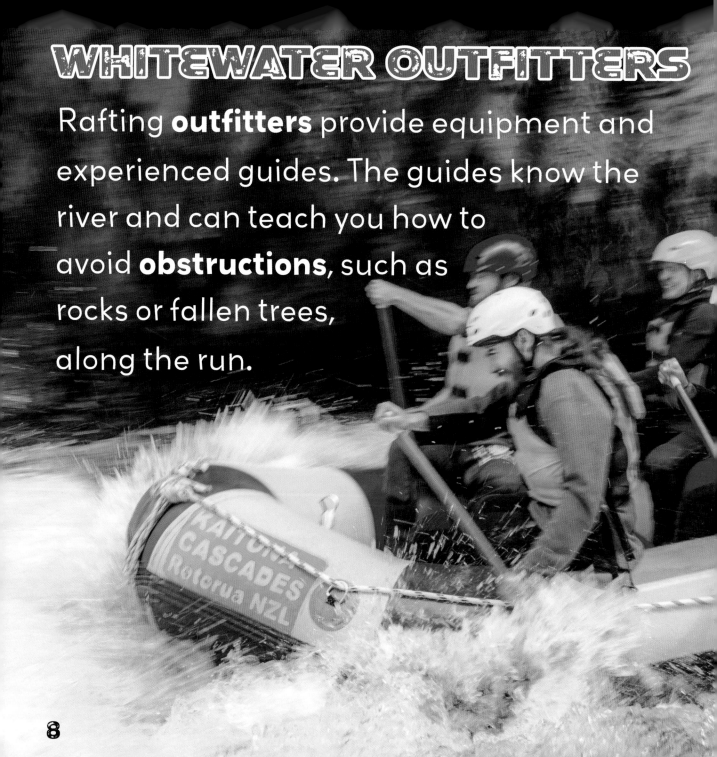

WHITEWATER OUTFITTERS

Rafting **outfitters** provide equipment and experienced guides. The guides know the river and can teach you how to avoid **obstructions**, such as rocks or fallen trees, along the run.

experienced guide

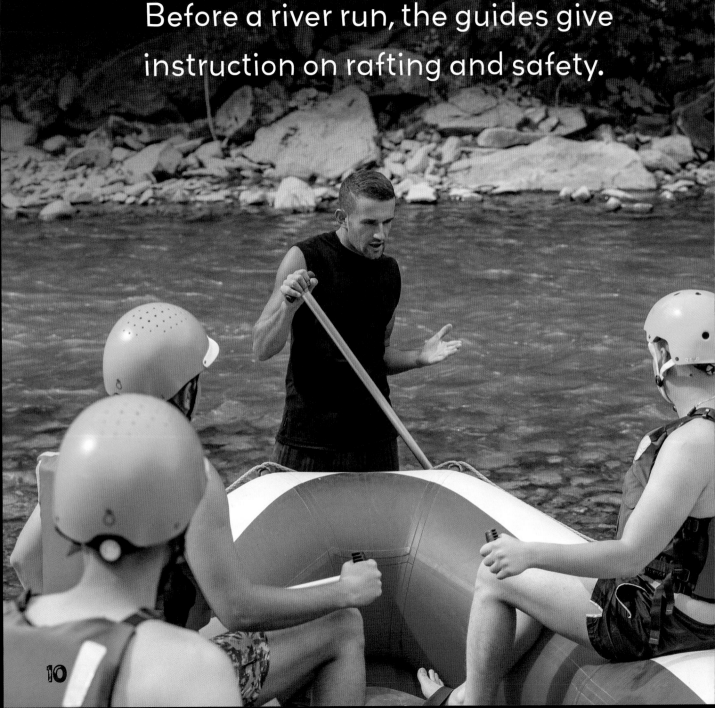

Before a river run, the guides give instruction on rafting and safety.

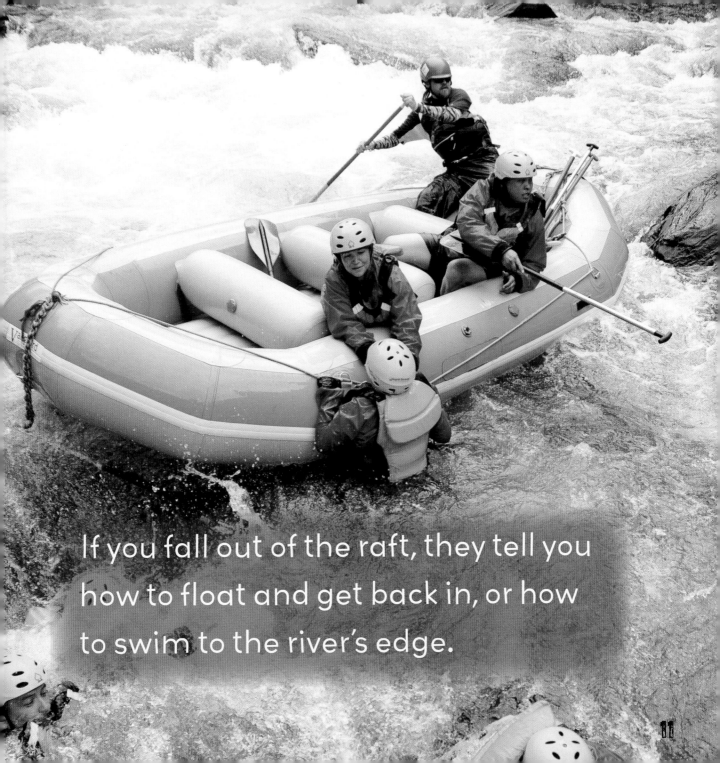

If you fall out of the raft, they tell you how to float and get back in, or how to swim to the river's edge.

RAFTING EQUIPMENT

An inflatable raft, paddles, oars, helmets, and personal flotation devices (PFDs) are basic rafting equipment.

A paddle can have a single or double blade. The paddler must hang on to the paddle and not lose it in the water.

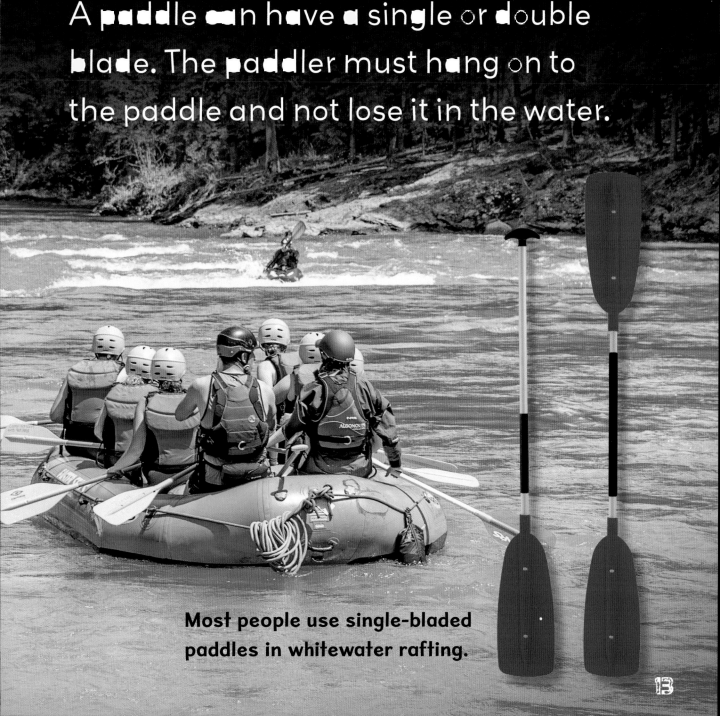

Most people use single-bladed paddles in whitewater rafting.

Outfitters supply the basic equipment, but you have to come prepared. You'll need sunscreen, a hat, sunglasses with a strap, and water shoes or sandals with straps.

It's a good idea to wear a swimsuit under your clothes. Your trip may include lunch and a swim on the river's edge.

RIVER RATINGS

River ratings are based on a river's difficulty and danger. Depending on the season, ratings can sometimes change.

There are six ratings:

Class 1 has moving water with little or no waves or obstructions.

Class 2 has fast water with waves and obstructions that require some maneuvering to be avoided.

Class 3 has waves, strong currents, and some small drops. Rocks or other obstructions take a lot of maneuvering to avoid.

Class 4 has powerful rapids, unavoidable waves, holes, and obstructions that demand fast maneuvering with experienced skill level.

Class 5 has long, obstructed, and violent rapids with drops, holes, and narrow chutes. Class 5 requires a high level of fitness and advanced skill.

Class 6 is for expert teams only. Class 6 runs are not used often because of unexpected dangers and difficult rescue situations.

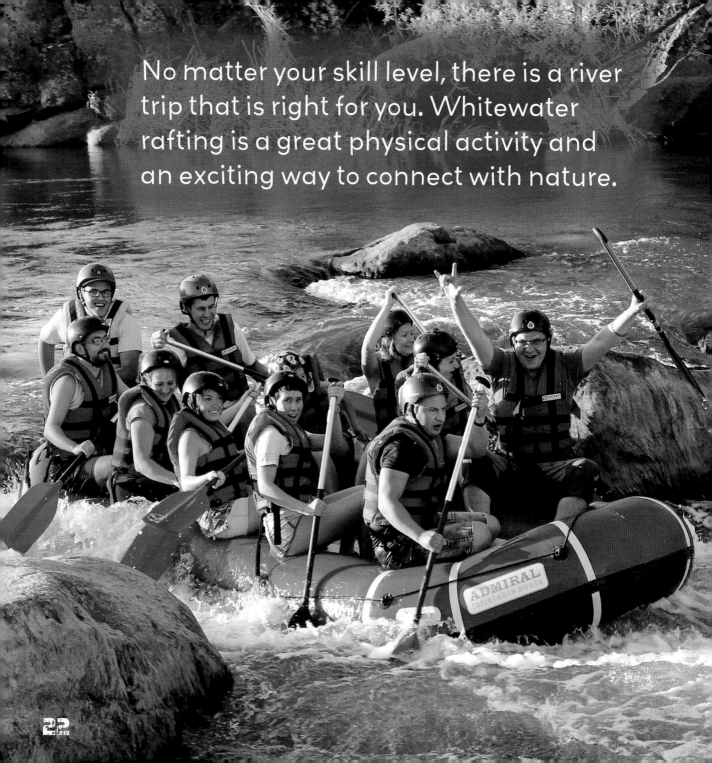

No matter your skill level, there is a river trip that is right for you. Whitewater rafting is a great physical activity and an exciting way to connect with nature.

GLOSSARY

chutes (SHOOTS): Narrow passages

maneuvering (muh-NOO-vur-ing): Performing a series of skilled movements

obstructions (uhb-STRUHK-shuns): Things in the way

outfitters (OUT-fit-urz): Businesses that provide equipment and services

rapids (RAP-idz): A place in a river where the water flows very fast

turbulent (TUR-byoo-luhnt): Moving unsteadily or violently

INDEX

School-to-Home Support for Caregivers and Teachers

This book helps children grow by letting them practice reading. Here are a few guiding questions to help the reader build his or her comprehension skills. Possible answers appear here in red.

Before Reading

- **What do I think this book is about?** I think this book is about how to be safe while whitewater rafting. I think this book is about the thrill of riding through a rapid in a raft.

- **What do I want to learn about this topic?** I want to learn more about the difficulty and danger ratings of rivers. I want to learn how old you must be to go whitewater rafting.

During Reading

- **I wonder why...** I wonder why whitewater rafting is done in inflatable rafts instead of boats. I wonder why some paddles have a single blade and why others have double blades.

- **What have I learned so far?** I have learned that whitewater rafting with your family or friends can be an exciting adventure. I have learned that to be safe while whitewater rafting you need a good guide and excellent gear.

After Reading

- **What details did I learn about this topic?** I have learned that PFDs are personal flotation devices that you should wear all the time when you're on a river. I have learned that I should keep away from Class 6 rivers as they are very dangerous, and only expert teams should go on them.

- **Read the book again and look for the glossary words.** I see the word *outfitters* on page 8, and the word *chutes* on page 20. The other glossary words are found on page 23.

Library and Archives Canada Cataloguing in Publication

Available at the Library and Archives Canada

Library of Congress Cataloging-in-Publication Data

Available at the Library of Congress

Crabtree Publishing Company

www.crabtreebooks.com   1–800–387–7650

Print book version produced jointly with Blue Door Education in 2023

Written by: David and Patricia Armentrout

Print coordinator: Katherine Berti

Printed in the U.S.A./072022/CG20220201

Content produced and published by Blue Door Education, Melbourne Beach FL USA. This title Copyright Blue Door Education. All rights reserved. No part of this book may be reproduced or utilized in any form or by any means, electronic or mechanical including photocopying, recording, or by any information storage and retrieval system without permission in writing from the publisher.

Photo Credits: Cover, PG 1 © Sergey Ryzhov/Shutterstock.com. Page 4 black and white photo © Dirk Pons, https://creativecommons.org/licenses/by-sa/3.0/deed.en   Following images from Shutterstock.com: Page 2 © Johnathan Esper, image across Page 2 and 3 © sunsinger, illustration Pages 4 and 5 © Flash Vector, Page 7 © Sergey Novikov, image across Pages 8 and 9 © Robert Crum. Following images from istock by Getty Images: graphic of rock behind text throughout book © Alyona Jitnaya, title page © gregepperson, Page 3 wooden sign © Marat Musabirov, Page 9 © gregepperson, image across Pages 10 and 11 © hyejin kang, Page 10 © Merlas, Page 12 © Alisha Bube, Page 13 © Ruslanshug, Page 16 © gregepperson, Page 18 © lzf, Page 19 © PauloResende, Page 21 (small photo of climber) © Ladanifer, Page 22 © Jareck. Following images from Dreamstime.com: image across Pages 6 and 7 © Piccaya, Page 11 and 14 © Auremar, Page 15 © Artem Zaytsev, Page 17 © Photobac, Page 20 (rope) © Lithiumphoto, image across Pages 20 and 21 © Vitaliy Mateha, Page 21 (carabiner and rope) © Andrii Vergeles

Published in the United States
Crabtree Publishing
347 Fifth Ave.
Suite 1402-145
New York, NY 10016

Published in Canada
Crabtree Publishing
616 Welland Ave.
St. Catharines, Ontario
L2M 5V6

Important Note: Any sport is safe only when all participants follow rules for safety. Please carefully review the safety tips in this book.